Little Chimp

Story by Jenny Giles
Illustrations by Rachel Tonkin

Here is Little Chimp.

Here is Mother Chimp.

Little Chimp is asleep up in the tree.

Mother Chimp is awake.

Here comes Mother Chimp.

Little Chimp wakes up.

"Oo-Oo-Oo!

Mother Chimp!

Mother Chimp!

Oo-Oo-Oo!"

Mother Chimp looks up at Little Chimp.

Here comes Mother Chimp.

Mother Chimp comes up to Little Chimp.